LOVE
WHO
YOU
ARE

This journal belongs to

Introduction

The heart is the sacred temple of the inner goddess. The heart is not bound by logic. The mind may believe certain steps are necessary, when the heart knows another way is not only possible, but preferable, as it will help us avoid unnecessary pitfalls and delays and learn skills that will be useful in the long term. Listening to and following the heart often means taking an unconventional and unique route in life. The guidance that emerges from this deep inner wisdom can be quite confronting to the part of us that wants ideas to make sense at a logical level before we act upon them. Following our heart often involves challenging preconceived ideas and letting go of self-imposed limitations. As our society is more driven by ego than wisdom, it often means living in a way many people will not support or understand and may even actively criticise or ridicule. One must have courage to live according to the inner truth of the heart.

The logical mind may consider such actions foolish or frightening. What if there is failure? What if we make a mistake? Yet, the feminine is not afraid of tripping and bumbling along the path of creative soul expression. She knows the colt is unsteady on its legs before it becomes a graceful and powerful horse. That is part of progress — growth cannot happen without some initial wobble. The divine feminine sees the beauty and courage in taking the steps, even when we aren't certain we will ever gain our balance and poise. She wants us to empower her with our trust. When we dare, she can do what she wants to do. That is, she can guide us to fulfil our divine potential.

When we decide to love our inner goddess, we are choosing to live a truthful, creative and authentic life. We are deciding to live according to the wisdom of our hearts, rather than through the fear and judgement of our minds or of society at large. We are choosing to live from trust, even when things feel challenging or uncertain — and, they will feel that way now and then! The sacred feminine is not afraid to lead us through the dark if that is what it takes for us to realise we have the strength and inner talents needed to fulfil our divine destiny. Loving our inner goddess means listening to, trusting and acting on the kickass wisdom that comes from within irrespective of what anyone else may feel about it.

The inner goddess has a light and a dark face. Her light teaches us to create and experience joy, happiness, love, peace and freedom. She urges us to express ourselves, to have fun, to enjoy life and to celebrate all we are given. She brings blessings and abundance, makes clear our self-worth and teaches us that taking pleasure in life can be a sacred act of devotion and gratitude.

The shadow of the goddess urges us to confront our fears — to enter willingly into the challenges we probably wish didn't exist at all! She urges us to have faith in our courage and ability to move through the darker times. She is an ally when we face a breakup, an illness, a challenge to our identity, a failure, or the loss of security, a loved one, a job or a friendship we thought we could count on. The dark face of the inner feminine is not cruel, angry or mean, but she *is* fierce! She is our sacred badass friend who encourages us to trust there is goodness at work, even in the darkness. When we are unable to immediately recognise it, she helps us to hold faith that at some point, we will finally realise something good came out of our challenges.

Her dark face teaches us not to be afraid of life. Sure, we may quake in our boots at certain prospects, but with trust in her, we can admit our fears and still be willing to grow through whatever it is we face. When we realise the Universe is on our side, we can boldly and confidently say, "I will get through this with wisdom to make circumstances work for the betterment of my soul so, with the help of the divine feminine, let's do this!"

Working with a journal is a powerful way to learn to recognise the inner guiding voice of the feminine. She might not make much logical sense, but when we are really feeling her, we will sense the truth in what is coming through. Not being able to justify or explain an instinct, is often a good sign we are bypassing the intellect and tapping into the deeper, intuitive wisdom of our hearts, which is her sacred realm.

Keeping a journal may seem so simple that you may wonder if it really does very much at all. But, look around at how many people are too frightened to trust their own intuition or struggle to recognise their inner truth, let alone live it. This often comes down to profound inner confusion and uncertainty due to a lack of mirroring as a child. When parents and other caregivers and authority figures lack the skills and awareness to be a healthy mirror for a child's emotional life, they will learn to doubt their own feelings and inner experiences. They will feel uncertain of whether their intuition has value. The child may learn that making other people happy and comfortable is more important than acknowledging their own truth or expressing a need for their own happiness. This is especially true if the child's sense of self goes against the needs, wants, hopes and other projections of their caregivers — that is, where the child is not allowed the autonomy to explore and delight in their own expression, but is shackled to become an extension, prop or support of others. Journaling is a corrective experience.

When you begin to journal, you reinforce your inner truths and you will come to recognise what you are actually feeling. These pages will be a consistent and non-judging space where your inner life can find expression. Journaling has tremendous value and can support you in making small but important choices as well as life-changing decisions.

When I was going through the breakup of my first serious relationship, I was in so much doubt. My partner wanted to stay together, but though I loved him, I felt a rising unhappiness and suffocation in the relationship. I felt like I needed more freedom to be able to grow. I was writing in my journal, before I had made the clear choice to leave, when I felt the urge to go back and read over the entries from several months and even a year earlier. I flipped through the pages and was shocked. There were musings I didn't recall writing, stating the exact same feelings I was still struggling to accept. I realised I had been experiencing the pain I was currently in for a very long time. It was as though a spotlight had been directed to my situation and I could suddenly see I wasn't *making things up*. This was a recurring pattern in the relationship, this was genuinely how I felt about it, and if I didn't act on those feelings, I would continue this way indefinitely! That was not something I could accept and so I made the decision to leave. I went through that painful process of liberation and healing, with my journal helping me navigate choices, stay true to myself and purge painful emotions like grief and fear along the way.

In honour of all my inner goddess has taught me, I simply had to joyfully share it with others. So, I created *Love Your Inner Goddess* — a little book of her wisdom which includes sacred music you can dance to at home, in a healing circle, on the beach, naked under the moon, in your garden or whatever else works for you! There are short, guided meditations, sacred rituals and affirmations you can use to connect with her as well as spiritual guidance to open you to your inner world where your inner goddess is waiting for you. I have also created a companion oracle deck with intuitive guidance, healing processes and beautiful art to deepen your connection to the sacred feminine. And now, here is the *Love Your Inner Goddess* Journal which you can use in conjunction with the other offerings or on its own. Either way, it will support the connection with the divine feminine wisdom that is already unfolding within your heart.

The five healing processes included in this journal are best done when you have set aside some time for yourself. They can be done relatively quickly, or you can go deep and take longer if you choose. It is best to turn off mobile phones and other devices, keep the lighting soft and wear comfortable clothing. A space where you can go into your journey and not be distracted by the external world will best support your healing as you work through each process.

I hope this journal will help you find your way through darkness to light, through light into depth, and most of all, through confusion into clarity. As you open this journal, may you open to the wisdom of your inner goddess — a lot of the time she may just remind you to be patient and to trust in your own soul process. May you know her grace and goodness and feel refreshed and rallied for your soul's unique journey.

Much love dear one, namaste,

Alana

The sacred feminine in you is ready to rumble! She doesn't want your inner light to be hidden. She will fight for your right to grow, to celebrate and to be free. Trust her guiding wisdom, even when it ruffles feathers.

If you want a life of passionate purpose, start with knowing, accepting and loving who you are as a person. As you love, respect and nurture your authentic self, your wise inner goddess will help you understand what is truly you and what is best cast aside.

Discover the sacred rebel within. Say no to the voices of fear and hate and become a voice for love, truth and wisdom. You have the power to choose how you want to feel and what you want to express in each moment, no matter what is going on around you.

Living as a soul, with truth, takes real courage in this world. We are often taught to follow the rules and are assured that if we do so, everything will be okay. Your inner goddess thinks that is a bunch of nonsense. She knows that allowing your spirit to be controlled by others will stop your soul from growing and make you a prisoner of other people's fear.

Your inner goddess wants so much more for you. She will show you how to be a loving rebel, to break the rules that go against your soul and change the game, so you are playing from the heart. She'll show you how to live the life that is meant only for you.

There are personal and global issues that need to be healed. Your inner goddess knows how to bring about healing change with love, playfulness, courage and dignity. She will always show you the truth, always believe in you (because she knows what you are capable of) and will guide you to live from the heart every step of the way.

Trust yourself.

Your purpose can require a lot from you. It can ask you to become the best version of yourself, to use all your talents and to develop some you didn't know you had along the way. It will also fill your heart with joy. Your purpose is worth the effort it takes to attain it.

It is hard to have a positive effect on a situation when we are confused by lies, manipulations, hidden agendas and other forms of deception. When truth is revealed, we have clarity. We see who we really are, what is really going on and what we need to do — or not do. Never fear the truth. You have nothing to be ashamed of. You are growing and learning, and ultimately, will find your way with wisdom and grace.

*Inner beauty is the truest form of beauty. When you are happy
with who you are, it lights you up from within and frees you from
wanting to be someone else. Inner beauty helps you live your life
with joy, love, openness and a generosity that attracts so many
good things into your world.*

Your inner warrior goddess has courage, wisdom and determination. She may feel fear or doubt, but she also has spiritual strength which shows itself as a willingness to keep going through dark times, fighting for what is good and true with hope in her heart. This is why she succeeds.

Courage is the willingness to act even when you feel afraid or uncertain.

Wisdom helps us look for ways to grow through a situation. Without wisdom, we judge, blame or turn away from what is before us. With wisdom, we find our way through challenge, gaining great learning and empowerment in the process.

Your self-belief needs revision when the old ideas of who you are and what you are capable of are not up to the challenge before you. You are ready and capable to conquer any challenge sent to you, but you may need to learn some things about yourself before you realise this.

Magdalene Priestess

Invoking the protection of the Divine Feminine

Soul medicine for when you have been abused, judged, criticised or shamed

Your divine feminine spirit needs to feel cherished, adored, loved and worshipped for all that she is and all that she offers. She has so much love to give through the intimate sharing of her innermost self and through connection, touch and the sacred pleasure of her body. She knows that physical expressions of love are a sacred gift of high value and worthy of appreciation and respect. They are not to be demanded, taken for granted, abused or criticised in any way. Some who lack wisdom may try to shame your divine feminine spirit and judge her gifts of physical love. Some may claim they are owed and that her gifts of love be provided on demand on threat of harm, rejection, withdrawal of support, or otherwise. This type of behaviour is always, without exception, unacceptable and a blasphemy against the goddess. You are worthy of respect, and you have the power to assert your value, your purity and your grace, no matter what has been or may be, no matter whether others understand or agree with you. Know that dignity is always yours by divine decree. You need only claim it for yourself.

You can use a red scarf or a pashmina as a veil in this ritual — you can also use your imagination. Place the red veil over your head and say, *"The red veil of love, created from the blood of the divine heart made flesh, cleanses and protects me now. Through this extraordinary grace, I am freed from the pain of judgement, betrayal and abandonment. I reclaim my feminine dignity. I accept and honour my sacred beauty."*

Rest with this sacred protection, feeling that your true self can never be harmed. Allow the vitality and warmth of your heart to fill and heal every part of your being. Relax. Trust that you are restored in the depths of your soul.

Success is inevitable when you choose not to give up until you get there!

Reassure your mind that your heart can show you how to live in a way that is amazing — and that it's safe to trust in that.

You are a wild child of the Universe, and your heart is showing
you the way to fulfil your divine destiny.

Give yourself permission to live a life that makes your heart happy.
The world needs your joy.

Don't let fear—yours or anyone else's—control you. You are your own person.
Know that trying to fit in is only for those who are afraid to stand out.

You don't need to be like anyone else.

Inspire others to overcome their fears by believing in the truth
of your heart and going after what you want with passion and
confidence. You are a badass — in a good way.

Be
Your
Own
HERO

You are meant to explore a world bigger than the one you currently know. It is going to happen. Trust in divine timing. Be open to what life has in store for you.

It's time to let yourself off the hook. Learning from your choices is easier if you stop punishing yourself whenever you feel you've made a mistake. Sometimes, the only way to learn what we need to know is from what didn't work out so well at the time. Forgive yourself. Have your own back. Be good to you.

When fearful, angry people lash out and try to hurt others because they cannot get past their own hurt, do not make it about you. Your heart knows how to love and protect you, while having compassion for the suffering that another may be feeling. Remember, you must be there for yourself, nurturing your own heart with plenty of love.

,

Choose who you allow to get close to you and be guided with care. Before we accept guidance or influence from another, we want to make sure they are living the kind of life and are the kind of person we aspire to be! Open yourself to learn from others, but always stay true to your own heart.

Sometimes you will be all class and at other times you'll wolf down your lunch like it's the last meal you'll ever eat. Those who accept themselves unconditionally will be able to accept you—all parts of you—unconditionally, too. Choose who you share yourself with carefully. You deserve to be, and to be loved for being, all of you.

Put yourself in positive places and with positive people. Take time to generate light within you through those things that feel healing for you. This can be time with animals, nature, art, relaxation, music, dance or meditation. Nurturing your light will help you trust what is happening within you and in your world.

Your heart is a portal for healing. The heart knows how to gain closure on emotional, psychological, physical and spiritual matters. It will show you the way through the unknown, faithfully navigating transitions to lead you towards the light of a new day. Don't worry so much. Trust yourself and listen to your heart. All is working out according to a deeper wisdom.

No matter what human errors you may make—and we all make plenty in every lifetime—you will always be encouraged, healed and comforted by the unconditional love of the Divine Mother. Everything will work out according to her grace. Trust in her and allow relief to enter your heart.

Being cool is about being content with who you are and refusing to be stereotyped by people with insufficient imagination. There's power in the freedom of not fitting in. You, rather than someone else, gets to decide how you want to live your life. Relish it!

Inner Mermaid

Claiming your creative soul voice

*For when life becomes dull and disconnected from the imaginative
and nurturing depths of your soul*

When you need help to trust in the unconventional, to tune in to your unique
vision or to find a new approach or fresh answer, it is time to connect with your
inner mermaid. This part of you thrives in deep, creative, healing waters of
intuition and imagination — and sometimes you need to swim in deeper waters of
mystery and meaning. In those deep places, you can commune with the sacred
and be nourished by the unfamiliar, the creative and the healing energy of the
vast spiritual realms. To deny this and remain on the surface of things will not
satisfy your soul. It would be like eating stale biscuits when what you really
hunger for is succulent fruit, sweet with juice.

Too much of what most people think is the 'real world' dries out your soul.
However, the soul needs mystery and magic to come alive, to create, to emanate
light. Yearning for magic is not immature or escapist. Those soul cravings are
the voice of your inner mermaid, rising from your oceanic depths. Her siren
song is the voice of your true desires. Trust that you are connected to worlds
beyond this physical reality, the worlds of spirit, healing, intuition, meditation
and creativity. When you are in touch with her, you will embody your feminine
freedom and spiritual independence to discover a rich inner life that fills you,
inspires you, gives you energy and makes you crazy with wild laughter at just

how beautiful, strange and unexpected life can be. Your inner mermaid helps fuel your soul with what really satisfies you, so you can feel at home in the deep waters of your own soul.

Imagine your inner mermaid can sing to you using whatever words or sounds she likes. Feel her honest voice rise from the depths of your soul. Let her sing to you—out loud or silently—to express deep truths. Listen to her with your spiritual ability of inner hearing. Whether it makes sense straight away or not, receive her siren song with unconditional acceptance and loving respect.

If you want to take some time to write, record, draw or dance her song, focusing on key words, images or feelings, do that now. Remember this is soul art and therefore it is to be received unconditionally, without judgement. It needs to be free to be whatever it wants to be — silly, playful, meaningful, life-changing, a break from the ordinary, all the above or something else altogether.

There's a place where you belong. Maybe you've found it? You may still be looking. It doesn't matter how long you take to find it. It does matter that you believe you deserve a real home for your beautiful heart and that you don't give up until you are there. Your soul tribe-your true spiritual family-are part of your divine destiny and you are a part of theirs.

Be respectful and loving to yourself as you choose what to take into your being. The physical nourishment, the emotional input, the books you read and the entertainment you choose, all have an impact on you. When you take something in, ask yourself if you feel better for the experience? Does it nourish your soul? The best food for your soul is that which increases love.

When you realise you are strong enough to save yourself–which you are–you never have to be afraid again.

There is no-one worth losing yourself over. You don't need permission to stand your ground, to honour your values or to walk away from what isn't right for you.

An affirmation for being your own hero: I know how to rescue myself. I am worthy of respect. I choose happiness for myself. I am willing to follow my inner voice. When I don't know what to do, I know the answer will come at the right time and in the right way. I trust life. Deep within, I know I am going to be okay and everything is working out perfectly.

If someone is saying negative things about you, or you are thinking
negative thoughts about yourself or anyone else, don't believe them
and don't sink to that level by lashing out. Instead, speak goodness
and the beautiful truth you want to affirm right now.

Use the positive power of your words, thoughts and intentions to override and replace the meanness, fear, hate or jealousy of anyone else. The goodness in you is more powerful than the badness in anyone or anything else.

Fear can make us try to force something that isn't quite ready yet. Don't try to impose a meaning or outcome prematurely. Don't think too hard! When it is time for you to act, you'll know it. It's okay to relax. Trust that clarity will come when the time is right.

You are going through this because you are ready for it — even if you think you're not. There is a loving reason for all of it — even if you cannot see that right now. Put your faith in the mystery. Trust that you have a bright destiny ahead.

Living a great life is not about competing with anyone else. Living a great life inspires others to do the same. It doesn't take anything away from anyone else. Go after what you want with a happy heart.

Truly respecting and taking pride in yourself requires you to feel good about the person you choose to be and the way you choose to live your life. Be an inspiration to yourself. You don't need to try to impress anyone. You have everything within to make yourself proud. It's time to be your own hero.

Being different doesn't mean being alone, but when you try to change yourself to fit into a stereotype you will lose your way and feel increasingly rejected or defeated. The Universe doesn't want you to be someone else. It wants you to be you! When you love yourself as you are, you open the way for others to love the real you, too.

Deep down you are a good kind of crazy. Your weird streak is a proverbial breath of fresh air, preventing unimaginative collapse into the boredom of sameness. You are a divine poster child for others who want to break free from conformity and be themselves unapologetically. The Universe will support you every step of the way — because it so enjoys you just being you.

Don't give in to despair or believe things will not work out. You are learning to trust that the Universe knows what it is doing. There are great and beautiful things meant for you, and no matter what appears to be right now, they will come to you in the perfect way and at the perfect time. Keep your faith in the light.

It's not wise to take advice from people who are invested in creating pain. You can have compassion for them, but you must not underestimate how their negativity can taint your trust in the Universe. The only thing that can trap you is the choice to follow the negative and give in to fear. Be at peace — the positive light in you is stronger than any darkness.

The Universe has a beautiful plan for your life.

TRUE
LOVE
IS
ETERNAL

Shaman of Skulls

Surrendering into transitions

For when letting go means opening to what is taking place, with wisdom

Relaxing with trust during times of change can be hard to do. Yet, it is often the way to release pain more swiftly, so we can begin to see the spiritual blessing we couldn't see, let alone be comforted by, when we were locked into a more fearful perspective. Sometimes we outgrow things, and even when we know things need to change, we do not always feel ready. This can apply to a relationship, a phase of your life or an identity that no longer suits you. Perhaps it relates to an inner ending that you cannot quite articulate, but you feel nonetheless. This is a symbolic death with a greater and loving purpose. To be able to go through this experience with wisdom and trust, we need to find the power of the shaman within.

A shaman is spiritually trained to overcome the fear of symbolic death. Instead of avoiding endings, the shaman willingly goes through them with the awareness that every ending is simply the other side of a beginning. The shaman knows endings happen when something new wishes to be born. The shaman knows this is ultimately for good and has compassion for the human mind that may feel uncomfortable and resistant to the process.

Even when we accept a change, and do so with gratitude, we can still feel uncertain, afraid, confused or try to cling to what is ending. These are natural human responses to loss — especially when we sense the loss is irreversible and life will never be quite the same again. Be patient with yourself, be kind, but also know new life is now happening for you according to a higher purpose and loving plan. Your life is meant to change at this time. There is something good here that is wanting to be born. Be encouraged. Accept the pain and you will find that it passes more quickly. From the ashes of this symbolic death, you shall rise again, ready and open to receive the blessing that is destined for you.

Place your hands lightly on either side of your head. Say aloud: *"This sacred skull holds the light of wisdom and shines unconditional divine love in all directions now."*

Use your fingertips to gently massage your head, all over. Include under your jaw, behind your ears and allow your head to feel relaxed. Do this for as long as feels good. You may also like to massage your neck, perhaps slowing down your breathing and then exhaling on a sigh several times.

Affirm to yourself: *"I am loved, and it is safe to trust in this process of change. I have the wisdom and courage to be here for myself, to accept my feelings and even my doubts, to let them rise and fall, whilst within my heart is a steady, constant anchor of love, wisdom and trust."*

Imagine, feel or perceive a beautiful light. This is the new way of life readying itself to be born as you go through this transition. You may like to close your eyes and imagine relaxing and basking in the beautiful light of that new life.

You don't need to adjust your dreams to fit what others say is realistic, sensible or practical. Why limit the power of the Universe with negative expectations? Listen to what your heart yearns for. Believe the Universe has put those desires there and will show you every step to take to fulfil them.

We need brave souls to shake up our cultural values, so we stop hurting ourselves and each other. You can decide what it really means to be beautiful, successful and worthy. That's how you take back control and disempower the toxic definitions created by others.

An active imagination can be used to create nightmares or dreams. There's no need to torment yourself! Let yourself be free to feel positive about your future and know that everything is going to be okay.

It's safe to let things unfold as they will. There's no need to question your vision or your intuition just because situations are not working out the way you thought they would. The Universe is a little bent — it has a sense of humour! But, ultimately, it is kind and knows the best way to accomplish all that needs to happen.

It isn't always easy for you to be patient, but you know the value of patience.
You know that sometimes you must wait. Life knows how to work things out.

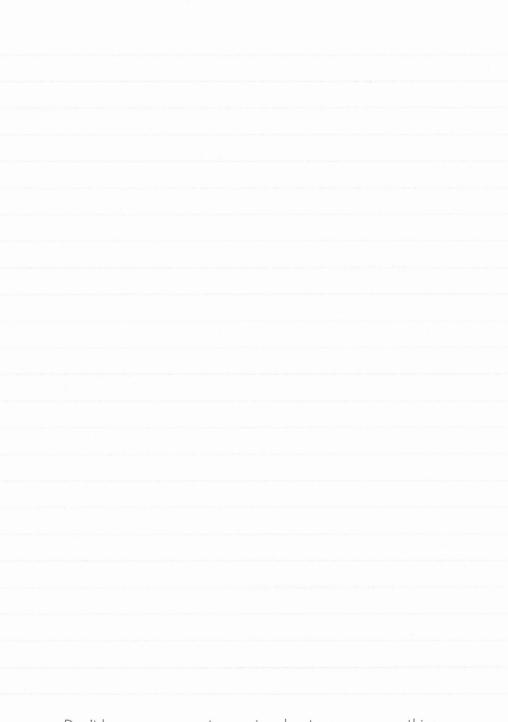

Don't lose your power to worries about anyone or anything.
Be at peace with yourself and life. When the time is right,
you will know what is true and what to do.

Rest is a way to prevent unnecessary suffering and to encourage much that is valuable. In restful quiet, we can hear our inner voice and the guidance of Spirit much more clearly. Getting enough rest helps us to live well.

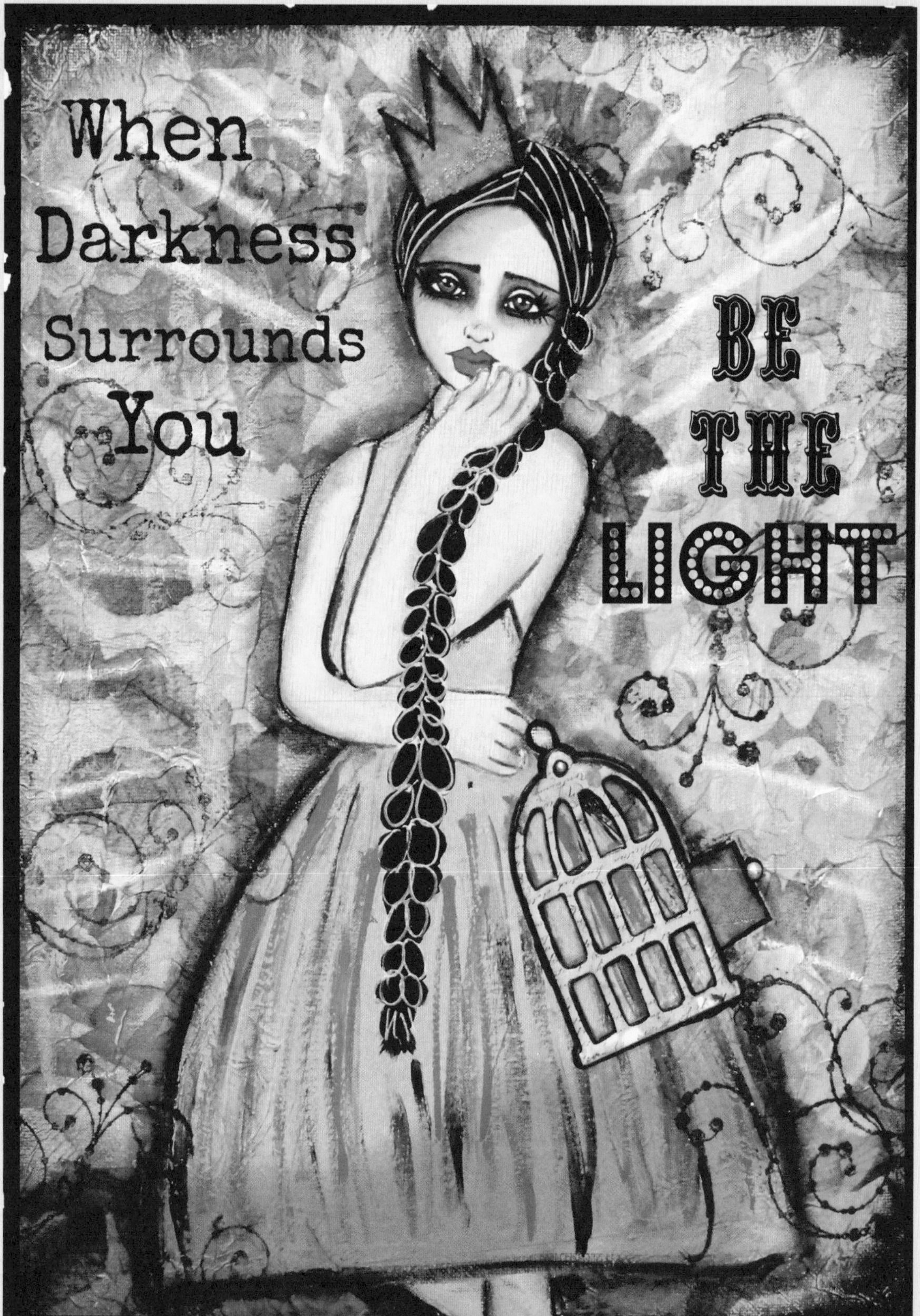
When
Darkness
Surrounds
You
BE
THE
LIGHT

Do you need some rest? You could imagine, feel, visualise or pretend that the Universe is holding you gently and safely in its hands whilst you lie back and relax.

The lioness within stands against beauty being used as a tool of manipulation to get something, to control someone, to put someone else down or to make them feel unworthy. She knows such behaviour is dishonourable – it distorts beauty into something ugly and corrupt. Lioness brings the soul medicine of respect so that beauty is not exploited but enjoyed and healing for all.

The generosity and power of the Earth Mother supports your wants and needs, helps you live your best life and fulfils your dreams beyond all you can imagine. She is already leading you towards your sacred purpose, providing exactly what is needed for your soul to blossom, just as she creates what is needed for the flowers of the earth to bloom.

If you have been beating yourself up, stop it now. Don't let anyone decide how you should feel about yourself. If you have done something you feel lacked integrity, do not damn yourself with judgement or allow another to steal your self-esteem. Take responsibility for your actions by doing something constructive and purposeful.

You are a dreamer, but you are also meant to be a doer.
Drop the distractions and go for it.

You can do it all, but not all at once. Trust your wisdom to set priorities and apply yourself, one step at a time.

Elk Medicine Woman

Steady does it, wild one

For patience, trust, and reassurance you are not falling behind as things are unfolding in the best possible way

Sometimes in our efforts to hustle and manifest, we can lose heart. A tantrum may rise from our bellies as we question whether the Universe is helping us at all! We can feel frustrated at delays or worry we aren't doing enough to manifest our dreams. Fear can start to take hold in our minds and we think things should be happening faster. The smallest obstacle could be taken as a sign our dreams are silly, we should grow up and get a real job or some such notion that creates further worry and confusion. Elk Medicine Woman helps us stop overthinking, so we can trust in divine timing. This trust brings us peace and helps us see that sometimes the steps we are already taking need time to create an effect. We don't give up on our dreams or our work. We do let go of the worry and fear which drains our energy and makes the journey so much less enjoyable!

Elk Medicine Woman comes with guidance to heal your soul, so you can maintain a pace that matches your inner rhythms. Do not feel rushed by urgency or external demands. You cannot force life to flow. The heart is at peace with this because it knows that perfect timing is divine timing. You have the endurance to go far and attain great things in this life. You must conserve your energy to maintain your stamina. If you push yourself to exhaustion, you just make the way harder for yourself. Nor does it speed up your results.

Forcing creates resistance which slows everything down. Elk Medicine Woman understands your great courage will take you to places others may not dare to go! With your inner wisdom and self-confidence, there is so much you shall achieve and receive. She whispers in your heart, affirming that your accomplishments shall be impressive. She guides you to work hard, but also to enjoy your life and allow others to support you. When divine timing is just right, you will hit your stride. You will attain all you have aimed for and more.

Place the backs of your hands on the top of your head with your fingers extending upwards in a slightly curved shape. These are your symbolic soul antlers! They draw in divine transmissions of guidance, blessing, energy and instruction. Imagine, visualise, feel or pretend that you can suction spiritual goodness into your soul antlers. Then, move your hands down to relax on your heart.

Affirm from the heart, *"I am wise and wild. My soul is growing in its own time. I open my heart to hope and trust. My heart nourishes my mind with peace and encouragement. I am growing steadily and authentically. I accept the perfection of divine timing with readiness, gratitude and joy."*

If you feel like using your soul antlers to playfully headbutt some doubts, fears and any other unknown invisible obstacles out of your way, do so now. Allow this silly sacred play to help you laugh and relax with trust in your heart.

You can experience complete rebirth, like a mythical phoenix rising from the ashes of what once was, with the past burned away. This is not about forgetting the past, but of breaking free of any hold it has over you.

The mind may believe it has the power to rule, but in truth, the heart is queen. Even when the mind doesn't want to surrender to the call of the heart-and fearfully lists numerous reasons the heart is crazy, stupid and its way will end badly-the doubt of the mind is no match for the power of the heart.

It is not your job to decide whether inspiration is practical, realistic or even possible. Let the Universe show off its creative flair for the unexpected and inspirational through you. Do not give up on what truly stirs your heart. Give the Universe an opportunity to make inspiration part of your world.

You might feel uncertain because you cannot see how something is going to work out. Know that the Universe is caring for you and will provide a way to move through this transition with grace.

Do not allow yourself to be shoved back into patterns of behaviour that are not true to who you are now. You have worked hard to grow and become this new self. Believe the new you is more real than the old you, even if she/he is less familiar to others (and maybe even to you) at this stage.

No matter how much pressure there is from the outside world or your own expectations, divine timing is ordering events so that what is meant to be, shall be. Balance the active pursuit of your dreams and ambitions with patience and trust.

Instead of fighting against life, feel it working with you and for you. Do what is within your power to do, but also pace yourself, trust and surrender.

You are going to find the exact help you need at the exact time you need it.

You can attract resources and even create something out of nothing.
Relax your mind and heart into the gentle expectation that you are
attracting all you need as you need it.

*Just like the emerging butterfly, the biggest challenges in our lives help
us to become what we were always destined to be.*

Sometimes, we need the Universe to push us to do what is needed to fulfil our divine potential. It's safe to trust what is happening in your life, even when the way ahead intimidates you.

You are one of the precious beings, not destroyed by, but able to find wisdom and empowerment through overcoming life's darker experiences. Everything that seeks to stop you just makes you stronger. You are a totally divine badass.

You have every right to feel bold and joyful about what life holds for you next.

You must stop torturing yourself with mean mind games. They are not good for you, and they are not true. When negativity threatens to put you down, let your soul speak from a place of feminine power and inner assurance as you say: I affirm myself. I am more than enough.

Black Diamond

Reclaim your inner light

For turning challenge into victory, deflecting negative energy and shining bright with refusal to be put down

Sometimes fear gets the better of people, and they feel small and want to tear others down to try to feel bigger. Have compassion for those people. Their darkness has (temporarily) got the better of them. If you feel like such people are slinging mud at you—and sometimes this can happen for those that shine bright—then it's time to reinforce your divine *badassery* and reclaim your fierce inner light. If you have been going through a dark time, brought on by others or your own inner fear or mental anguish, do this exercise to reconnect with Spirit and feel strong and peaceful again.

Black Diamond is the bearer of powerful spiritual mojo. She shines with dark beauty through the soul that has been able to withstand great intensity and remain intact. With the power to defend you against jealousy, ill-wishing and curses, Black Diamond gives you the power to face fear and not crumble beneath it. Your soul has been working with Black Diamond to transform your attitude towards fear, so you can acknowledge it without being overcome by it. Black Diamond is only available to the soul who is ready for it. It can take many lifetimes to be able to confront fear directly with peace and wisdom, without judgement, without allowing it to dominate you. Only when you have developed unconditional spiritual trust can you go through the darkness of the unknown and face your fears—or the fears of others—willingly. You must have trust, be certain you will learn something of value to your soul and know you will find your way out into the light once more. Your soul has that.

You are strong enough to experience the darkness within you and in the world around you, without breaking your trust in Spirit. You know it is just part of life and doesn't take away from the peace, beauty and power of divine grace. Your soul knows all is well. Even when we cannot see how, all things ultimately work for good. Black Diamond reminds you that you are an ancient and wise soul, with the power to create love out of darkness. You are made stronger through every experience. The things that once would have caused you pressure will become so much easier for you to handle. You are ready for the empowered, beautiful and precious life journey ahead.

Imagine, feel, visualise or pretend you have a black diamond resting in your hands. Say aloud, *"I call upon the deva of black diamond, and I give thanks for your protection, blessing and empowerment. Love and light will conquer all else."*

Imagine you are slowly releasing any fears or doubts into the black diamond, where they can be transformed into light. Imagine the inner goddess or deva of the black diamond munching up all your troubles and growing more powerful as she does so. She shines with a beautiful black light that absorbs fear. This sacred feminine void receives all and creates space for growth. When you are ready, imagine releasing the stone from your palms, allowing it to be slowly absorbed into the earth where it will remain, waiting for whomever needs it, at any time.

Take a moment to feel a connection with the light in your heart. It is always there. Sometimes the lampshade may get a little dirty from the hustle and bustle of life, but you can always imagine throwing that lampshade into a sacred fire and letting the inner light burn free and true. It can never, ever be extinguished. It is always there for you.

Sometimes, the lies we are repeatedly told become so familiar that we forget they are lies. Believing they are real is like poison for the soul. The soul needs truth like your body needs air. Give yourself permission to be truthful with your own soul and live honestly, authentically and bravely in this world.

Place one hand lightly at your throat and say the following aloud:
I now release any lies, gossip, curses or deceptions made by me or
against me, in this or any lifetime. Through divine love, mercy and
compassion, my entire being is now blessed and cleansed. I am free to
live, love and express truth in all its shining glory.

Say this prayer aloud: The Madonna of Roses blesses me with the wisdom to share myself with those who truly love me. I forgive those who have tried to use me, and I forgive myself for allowing myself to be used. Now, it is time to start anew, with strong thorns of protection. My rose soul blooms for all to behold.

To live the dream, we must surrender the fantasy. This can be painful. It feels like the end — when, in fact, it is the beginning. The pain passes, and we know the joy of having what we yearned for come to life.

When we are stuck in our heads, we only believe what we can see and know right now. This is unnecessarily limiting. Your heart can attract wonderful opportunities and special connections that you haven't even imagined yet.

Forgiveness frees you from what has been and allows you to open to something new, wonderful and different in your life. Forgiving may seem like freeing another, but it is the person doing the forgiving who attains freedom.

Overcoming the fear of what others think is usually one of the first things that happens as we start to play. It brings us an incredible freedom to be who we are without apology or fear. It opens us to the healing experience of being loved and accepted for who we really are.